Yellow Tree Alone

Selected Poems

Marlene Hitt

Yellow Tree Alone

Selected Poems

Marlene Hitt

Moonrise Press, 2023

COPYRIGHT INFORMATION

Yellow Tree Alone. Selected Poems by Marlene Hitt is a book of poetry published by Moonrise Press. P.O. Box 4288, Los Angeles – Sunland, CA 91041-4288, www.moonrisepress.com.

© Copyright 2023 by Moonrise Press and Marlene Hitt. Cover design by Maja Trochimczyk based on a photograph by Karen Winters. Used by Permission. Prior publication of certain poems in other books and journals is acknowledged, with copyright by Marlene Hitt.

No part of this book may be reproduced or utilized in any form or by any means, electronic or mechanical, including photocopying and recording, or by any information storage and retrieval system, without permission in writing from the publisher.

Manufactured in the United States of America

The Library of Congress Publication Data:

Hitt, Marlene (b. 1936) – author.

    [Poems. English.]

Yellow Tree Alone. Selected Poems / Marlene Hitt, author

182 pages (xviii pp. prefatory matter, and 164 pp.); 6 in x 9 in. Written in English, with one portrait.

ISBN 978-1-945938-34-4, paperback

ISBN 978-1-945938-35-1, ebook in ePub format

10 9 8 7 6 5 4 3 2 1

Contents

Acknowledgement by Marlene Hitt ~ x
Preface by Alice Pero ~ xii
In Appreciation by Dorothy Skiles ~ xiv
Publisher's Note by Maja Trochimczyk ~ xvi
Prior Publication Credits ~ xvii

Chapter 1. That Silken Whisper ~ 3
1. Humankind ~ 4
2. A Meditation ~ 5
3. I Wonder ~ 10
4. Give Way ~ 11
5. If I Knew ~ 13
6. If I Had Known ~ 14
7. Up and Over ~ 15
8. At a Campfire ~ 16
9. The Whisper ~ 18
10. The Music ~ 19
11. Back and Forth ~ 20
12. Prophecy ~ 21
13. Question ~ 22
14. Yes, I Grieve ~ 23
15. Success, Fame ~ 24

Chapter 2. Threads ~ 25
16. A Long Thread ~ 26
17. Threads, the Children ~ 27
18. Thread One ~ 28
19. Voyage ~ 30
20. Going Home ~ 31
21. Everywhere ~ 32

22.	Shawl ~ 35	
23.	Smoke Rings ~ 36	
24.	Healing ~ 37	
25.	Who is She, My Mother ~ 38	
26.	All about Ashes ~ 41	
27.	My Mother Visits ~ 42	
28.	Mother's Day 1998 ~ 43	
29.	Take Me Away ~ 44	
30.	Scent of Mystery ~ 46	
31.	Tell Me a Story, Daddy ~ 47	
32.	Curiosity ~ 48	
33.	Homecoming ~ 50	
34.	Great Grandfather's Reply ~ 51	
35.	More Than the Parts ~ 52	
36.	The Landmark ~ 53	
37.	A Story ~ 54	

Chapter 3. Along the Path ~ 55

38.	New Year on Canvas ~ 56	
39.	Devil Wind ~ 57	
40.	What the Thunder Said ~ 58	
41.	What Could You Do with a Bubble ~59	
42.	Take it Back ~ 60	
43.	Enlightenment ~ 61	
44.	Guilt ~ 62	
45.	The Grown Up Year ~ 63	
46.	Flowers ~ 64	
47.	Reveries ~ 65	
48.	The Real Reason ~ 66	
49.	As a Fly Buzzes By ~ 67	
50.	Walls ~ 69	

	51.	The Glass ~ 70
	52.	Catatonia Stone ~ 71
	53.	Collision ~ 72
	54.	Thought Fermentation ~ 73
	55.	Cleaning out the Past ~ 74
	56.	Caged Things ~ 75
	57.	Here I Lie Still, ~ 76

Chapter 4. Fallen Words ~ 77

	58.	Puzzling ~ 78
	59.	New to New ~ 79
	60.	How Far Have I Come? ~ 81
	61.	Fibril Underneath ~ 82
	62.	Night Lights ~ 84
	63.	Topography Map ~ 86
	64.	Child on the Floor with a Marble ~ 87
	65.	I Missed You ~ 89
	66.	Fallen Words~ 90
	67.	New Box of Crayons ~ 91
	68.	Echo ~ 92
	69.	All This ~ 93
	70.	The Word ~ 94
	71.	Darkness ~ 95
	72.	The Day the Poets Were Silent ~ 96
	73.	Love Poem ~ 97
	74.	If I Knew Your Name ~ 98
	75.	No Listing in the Yellow Pages ~ 99
	76.	Where Will I Put the Keys ~ 100
	77.	To the Stones ~ 101
	78.	Bulky Item Pick Up ~ 102

Chapter 5. Thunder Under the Ground ~ 103

79.	Two Times Around is a Mile and a Half ~ 104	
80.	The Fire That Drinks the Water ~ 105	
81.	This Mad Journey ~ 106	
82.	Ripples ~ 107	
83.	River Cutting ~ 108	
84.	Color of the Mind ~ 109	
85.	Oaks ~ 110	
86.	Cremation of the Sycamore Tree ~ 112	
87.	All Beautiful and Treasured Things ~114	
88.	Prayer of Thanks ~ 116	
89.	Disaster ~ 117	
90.	Memories ~ 118	
91.	A Cloud Passed Moon ~ 119	
92.	Spine Flower ~ 120	
93.	Musings about Walls ~ 121	
94.	Rock, Bush, Sand ~ 122	
95.	Blind Born Fish ~ 123	
96.	In Any Forest ~ 124	
97.	Intersection ~ 125	
98.	Death Dances ~126	
99.	Deep in the Spring ~127	
100.	My Very Own Place ~ 128	
101.	This Romance ~129	
102.	It Wasn't Always This Way ~ 130	

Chapter 6. The Web ~ 131

103.	Cards at Midnight ~132
104.	Green and Cresting ~ 133
105.	Homeless ~134

106.	Thorns ~ 135	
107.	Naming the Garden ~ 136	
108.	That Day ~ 137	
109.	The Gallon of my Life ~ 138	
110.	Wasp ~ 139	
111.	Green ~ 140	
112.	The Web ~ 141	
113.	The River of Time ~ 142	
114.	All the Way Down ~ 143	
115.	Now I Can Hear the Plodding of Beetles ~ 144	
116.	To J. Alfred Prufrock ~ 146	

Chapter 7. Pillars of Motes ~ 147

117.	The Wind is The Wind ~ 148	
118.	After ~ 150	
119.	Dust to Dust ~ 151	
120.	Underneath ~ 152	
121.	Need the Light ~ 153	
122.	Old Ones Gone Away ~ 154	
123.	No Words ~ 155	
124.	No Poem ~ 156	
125.	I Wish for You ~ 157	
126.	Hummingbird ~ 158	
127.	As the Hawk Flies ~ 159	
128.	Bury Me ~ 160	
129.	Yellow Tree Alone ~ 161	

About Marlene Hitt ~ 163

Acknowledgment

No poem emerges alone but is the product of many influences. Mine have come from years with the Chupa Rosa Writers, The Village Poets and from the influence of many other individuals. For this selection I thank the beauty around me, the work of other poets, of song writers and novelists whose words I admire. I thank my friends and family; the children who have taught me how to see.

More specifically, I thank Alice Pero who found my great stack of poetry, whose eyes saw and whose heart connected with my thoughts. Alice chose those she found worthy and arranged them in order and in the appropriate spaces. I am always grateful to Maja Trochimczyk who, with her expertise as publisher has made possible the work of many to be seen and appreciated, and whose support has made firecrackers of my enthusiasm.

I thank the Village Poets and Bolton Hall Museum for these many years of happiness, especially the Laureates: Joe, Pam, Elsa, Katerina, Damien, Ursula, Maja, Alice, and Dorothy whose gift is to unpack a poem to fully fathom its meaning. Thelma Reyna has been the gift of a friend. I am grateful too to Genevieve Krueger of the Chupa Rosa Writers who gave me a better education in literature than any university course. We will never forget her.

It takes many minds, many more than I can say here to influence any work. They are all a part of me and of my words.

Marlene Hitt
25 March 2023

Preface

Some people, wise or not so wise, seek to put poets in boxes and categories. This one is "academic," that one "beat," another "confessional" and then there is the "ecstatic." But reading Marlene Hitt's work is like coming into a room with poems of all colors. She is both conscious and unconscious. Her poems come from deep memory which contains the pioneer, the American Indian, the American housewife, the howls of coyote and the silent slither of snake. We find the landscape of Sunland-Tujunga, dry and rocky, powerful and mystical all at once. We find the solidity of the "real" and the ephemeral of the spirit world.

 She "sits before us" without excuse or modesty, a person who does not hide her doubts and confusions as she says in *A Meditation,* "Yet I am A new universe/ a Shy mutant/I am/ A confusion/I am/Unsolved And in the same poem, Here I sit before you/Eyes the color of an echo,/Skin pretending to look wise,/ An ordinary room in a/House of un-ordinary/Dimension." As a poet she can conceive of her eyes being "the color of an echo" and so we realize she will never be in any "ordinary" room; she is extraordinary. These poems are history, threads through her own life mid-20th century when women still embodied home. She struggled with her differences, never able to really "fit," yet always able to love. She writes of her father, mother: "Who is she, my mother?/A genius with wool and threads/ Oblivious to a poem…"grandparents, great grandparents, husband. But she is never without doubts. Do they know that under the floorboards, under the table laden with bounteous food, heads bowed in prayer, "under our feet, below the wood and slab/there would be hardened prints/of warriors? /Pieces of rusted knives,/black arrowheads/a lost flintlock…What would be the purpose of the prayers?/Or the wars?"

Her poems take us through known history, back to pre-history, to gods of the past, to stories she has found and reinvented. In these marvelous poems. Hitt is an observer; she reflects life, a mirror with words. Her poem, "Everywhere" that previously gave rise to the title of her first Moonrise Press book, *Clocks and Water Drops* (2015) has the flavor of Walt Whitman flying through the world, as she repeats the refrain… "Water drips in a London flat," she travels "everywhere," asleep, yet totally awake as she wanders, seeing all the tiny things that make life something worth wandering through. "Scree falls in Utah/falls on a silenced beetle/just one B flat howls in Sylmar/an intruder is caught/a stone skims on Lake Victoria/close to shore… everywhere there is movement/please that it shall never stop."

Find these poems and wake up. Marlene Hitt's voice is movement and thunder and it will never stop.

~ Alice Pero

In Appreciation

I'm so pleased that this rich collection of poems is in print. Almost 30 years ago, I joined a small poetry group in the Sunland-Tujunga area and that's when I met Marlene Hitt. She became the first Poet Laureate of Sunland-Tujunga serving a 2-year term 1999-2001. Over the years, we have become close friends. Her love of poetry and service to the community have been an inspiration to me and many others. In 1999, Marlene studied poetry at Trinity College in Dublin, Ireland and as a result of her experience, she wrote a number of poems. When she returned to the States, I read the poems and responded with a poem and so began an "email volley." The result was a collaborative chapbook entitled *Riddle in the Rain* (2003). Over the last ten years, as members of the Village Poets of Sunland-Tujunga we have collaborated with the Little Landers' Historical Society to provide a place for seasoned poets and new poets to read their poems and a place where the public is welcomed.

    Marlene's new collection of poems, highlights her gift as a storyteller. Many of her poems are in narrative form. Sounds of life in all of its forms speak to us in her poems: *Everywhere*, "water drips in a London Flat/a canary sings in Paris...". *The Music*, "music fell, the little notes, .../ dropping much like snowflakes/drifting everywhere." *What the Thunder Said:* "thunder shouted with/dry/deep voice.../"no more," he rumbled! /no more!" *Oaks:* "...the sound of the ax/the sound of the saw/eats into my sleep/with its open maw." And *Wasps*, "...speak in whispers/and pray/in their own words."

Threaded throughout Hitt's poems is a deep love of nature. Throughout this collection, her observations of the natural world are best understood if "I ...speak their names/savor the sounds my lips make." In *Naming the Garden*, Marlene observes that "Bushes with plain and simple leafy life/reveal themselves and I speak their names/savor the sounds my lips make." *In All Beautiful and Treasured Things*, the poet states: "I fly/over wild buckwheat, ..." / "...touch the wild rose" /"My temple stands among the flowers of the chuparosa." In *Cremation of the Sycamore Tree*, the poet mourns the cutting down of so many trees. Her litany of "never love a tree," runs throughout the poem. "It's not wise to love a tree/that interfere with men/Watch the smoke of sycamore form/smoke lifts as if to mourn."

Her portrayals of human relationships are both honest and poignant, including poems about her mother and father and others that have passed on. Glimpses of family relationships are found in many poems, for instance in *Echo:* "I hear my mother's voice/and the coughs and curses/of my father/and all those whispers/from the ages past." In *Smoke Rings*, "The grave lies open for my father's death/I curl his coat around and smell/the smoke rings tangled there/think of them over his curly hair/he left too soon. I loved him well."

Finally, In *Bury Me*, the poet tells what she wants to be buried with: "a leaf from the cottonwoods, the seed of an oak, a vessel of stones, a feather from the road, "...Then touch your hand/to my lips/that I may taste love on my journey."

~ *Dorothy Skiles*

Publisher's Note

I am delighted to share with readers this new collection of 129 poems by Marlene Hitt, written over a period of almost 40 years. The first Poet Laureate of Sunland-Tujunga, member of Chuparosa Poets, Village Poets, and other poetry groups, Marlene Hitt practiced her writing in near isolation from the "official" poetry world, while dedicating her time to the local community, as a historian, poet, and activist. As a sixth Poet Laureate of Sunland Tujunga, member of the Village Poets, and co-editor of our 10th anniversary anthology *We Are here: Village Poets Anthology* (2020), I am profoundly grateful for Marlene's collaboration and dedication to poetry. Her work was in almost all our anthologies. As the publisher of Moonrise Press, I am even more grateful for her poetic insights, her gifts of keen observation, reflection, and vivid expression. In 2015, it was my great pleasure to select poems for *Clocks and Water Drops*, her first full-length poetry volume. The current collection reprints some of these poems, and gathers other work scattered in various publications over the years. But there are plenty of poems here that never saw the light of the day and are here to enlighten and inspire us. I am thankful to Alice Pero for the enormous effort of selecting poems from thousands of pages and arranging them into seven chapters with distinct moods. In collaboration with Marlene, I changed the title of the whole volume from the *Thunder Under the Ground* proposed by Alice, into a more euphonious *Yellow Tree Alone*, that shines with the gold leaves of Marlene's unique talent.

~ *Maja Trochimczyk, Ph.D.*

Prior Publication Credits

Prior publication of certain poems is gratefully acknowledged:

Crystal Fire. Poems of Joy and Wisdom, edited by Maja Trochimczyk (Moonrise Press, 2022): *Color of a Brisk and Leaping Day, What am I Thankful For? Echo, Field Trip with the Sixth Grade, Boxes*

Clocks and Water Drops, by Marlene Hitt (Moonrise Press, 2015): *Threaded Thoughts, Night Lights, Tell Me A Story, Broken, Everywhere*

California State Poetry Society Blog and Poetry Letter No. 1 of 2022, winners of CSPS Monthly Contests for January, 2021, posted on the blog on 6 April 2021: *Summer of Fire.* https://www.californiastatepoetrysociety.com/2021/04/monthly-contest-winners-january-march.html

California Quarterly, Vol 44, No. 1, Spring 2018, edited by Maja Trochimczyk: *Enlightenment, Waiting Peaceful Journey, Bury Me*

Coiled Serpent. Poets Arising from the Cultural Quakes & Shifts of Los Angeles, edited by Luis J. Rodriguez et al. (Tia Chucha Press, 2016): *Child on the Floor With a Marble*

Altadena Poetry Review, edited by Pauline Dutton and Elayne Lipkin (2018): *Bury Me*

Chuparosa Calendar Diaries (Chuparosa Writers, 1992, 1993, and 1994): *Hummingbird, If I Knew Your Name, Guilt, Death Dances,* and *Spineflower Blues*

Meditations on Divine Names, edited by Maja Trochimczyk (Moonrise Press, 2012): *St. Andrews in the Rain, Prayer of Thanks*

Serenity Press, Chuparosa Writers, 1999): *Blues, Blue, What Would This Mean?, A Long Thread , No Words, Puzzling*

Night Birds, edited by Elsa Frausto (Chuparosa Writers, 1993): *After, Death Dances Best, Eclipse*

Sad With Cinnamon, a Chapbook (1999): *Threads, the Children, Walls, Threaded Thoughts*

Time Capsule buried at Sunland Park, July 4, 2000 (technically not a publication): *River of Time*

Riddle in the Rain, chapbook by Marlene Hitt and Dorothy Skiles, 2003: *Journey, All the Way Down, As Hawk Flies, Prophecy, Up and Over*

Sometimes in the Open, Poems from Southern California Poets Laurate, 1999): *Puzzling*

Verdugo Verses (California Federation of Chaparral Poets, John Steven McGroarty Chapter, 1990): *Looking Back, Reveries, Bury Me*

Village Poets Blog, June 23, 2021: http://villagepoets.blogspot.com/2021/06/round-robin-in-circle-summer-poetry.html: *Two Times Around is a Mile and a Half, Need the Light*

Voice of the Village monthly community paper, Shadow Hills newsletter, and *Clocks and Water Drops: The Plodding of Beetles*

We Are Here: Village Poets Anthology, edited by Maja Trochimczyk and Marlene Hitt (Moonrise Press: 2020): *Love Mended, Enlightenment, Color of a Brisk and Leaping Day, Green and Cresting*

When the Virus Came Calling, edited by Thelma T. Reyna (Golden Foothill Press, 2020): *Regrets*

Yellow

Tree

Alone

Chapter 1

That Silken Whisper

Humankind

Oyez, oyez, don't rise!

We are gathered here today
in the presence of our animosities
dearly beloved
to gather together passions
with words and words
to collect all the words.
Write them down.
We are gathered together
to share our prevailing stories
with attitudes and critical comments.
Strike that!
We are gathered here today
dearly beloved to join together
these words and these people
to unite, to bond together, make one
in acceptance that all creatures
are created equal
in the mighty presence of God.
May his angels watch over us
as we continue to be
that which and who we are,
Amen and amen.

A Meditation

I.

I am
My past
I am
Ghostly thoughts
I am
A sliver of memory
Festering in a thousand minds
I am
Parts and pieces of ancestors
Yet I am
A new universe
A shy mutant
I am
A confusion
I am
Unsolved

II.

A little boy kissed me on the
Cheek one day.
The kiss dried and blew away.
I did not believe in love.

Once, an acorn necklace
Made by the blistered fingers of a
Red-haired boy
Symbolized my acceptance of a
Ninth summer pledge of
Marriage.

Another day
I wrapped away the letters from
A young soldier coming home
From Korea.
We were married on a hot
September night and we lived
Happily ever after.

III.

I was a child who asked the sun
Where I came from and why.
Bright blue eyes and sky looked
Back and forth at each other.
I was a little girl who had red marks
On the backs of her legs because she
Sassed. Again.

One day I saw that my body had
Betrayed me.
It had become
Something I could barely
Live within.

My real world, full of lavender dreams,
Was in my mind.
My real home was in the spirit trees and
Shadow waterfalls. In the darkness,
Invisible arms wrapped me with love.
I wanted Bambi's mother instead of
My own.

The creatures of my heart,
Real creatures, died. I
Buried them with pieces of
Farewells in their graves and
Mourned them.

My teacher made me write a poem.
She liked it, made a newspaper around it.
Everyone else had to write a poem then to
Fill the empty spaces.
She made thirty copies from a slab of gel.

I watched my father from
My smallness. He mixed elixirs,
Weighed powders.
I smelled barrels of yeast tablets,
Tasted gelatin capsules when they were
New and unused. In the drug store
I hid in shame as grown-ups whispered
About bodies and
Secret things and my mother said
"Shhh not here, not now."

IV.

What am I?
I am
Silver wind in moonlight
I am
A lumpy monster breathing
Bad breath
I am
A moth flitting to a flame
I am
A slug resting in darkness
I am
Quick and Easy #106 and
Revlon coral #42
I am
Tea time with Haviland
A wine-toast from a paper cup
I am
Earth and fire, water and shadow
Sometimes sunshine falls on the past
Sometimes snow, sometimes
Hoarfrost cracks its branches

V.

Here I sit before you,
Eyes the color of an echo,
Skin pretending to look wise,

An ordinary room in a
House of un-ordinary
Dimensions.
My roots are twined in bedrock,
My feet mired in the quicksand of
My own making.
I am trapped in the sand and mud,
My boots too heavy to lift.

VI.

I am
A past
I am an
Image soft and faded
I am
A thought dying away
I am
An unfinished equation
After days and days and days
My past
Will cease

I Wonder

I wonder what joy is
And where is death.

I wonder about the newborn babe
And its one and only breath.

I wonder where love goes
When it steals away,

And the place where the years go
Day by day.

Give Way

Yield to the row of big rigs passing
at seventy miles an hour,
to kittens crossing the road,
to the warm hollow in your bed.

Give in to the current in the wide river
that flows forever, lets you in
for a short ride. Yield to sunrise
and the setting of the sun at half-past four.

Stand aside for the big woman edging in front
of you
and the locking of doors; give way
to small arms stretching no matter whose
and old ladies who have temper tantrums.

Give way to the earth which carries you
around.
To marshy edges and the bear's habitat.
Give your heart to snowflakes on black
and prism rainbows on the kitchen cloth.

Yield to those who are so sure
that cows are blue and earth is flat,
and all the loud voices that free you
to rest in the shadows.

Give way to the shallow cup and lukewarm tea
kettles boiling dry as the breeze blows your hair
and to all that is free, ignore all charges,
and do go gentle into that good night

If I Knew

for certain
where I was going
the hour of arrival
the weather there
I would know how to pack
know what raiment I would need
what thoughts I should carry.
This road defies the compass
leads into darkness so thick
no one could see through it.
Will I walk, or fly?
Ride a riptide?
Be rowed across a river?
Will I flow to the
wrong end of the earth?
In fear, I slip into a hiding place
face backward
put my hands over my eyes
wait for forever.
Or, study. Learn about all heavens.
Join the congregation, then
trudge toward the one whose heaven I like
best.

If I Had Known

If I had known
    about the burning rock,
    about the plains dry dust,
    about the elephant's habitat,

If I had known
    about the tears and pain,
    about children's rotted faces,
    about flies on starving lips,

If I had known
    about the pain of cold
    felt deep in doorways
    and loneliness beneath bushes,

If I had known
    about trembling earth,
    about old men clutching a handful of
    all they kept of life,

If I had known…

but

    I did know.

Up and Over

The way the path leads up and over,
up and over again and again
on this dry and stony land
there are no footprints to follow,
no strips of cloth or scratches in sand.
The spider burns her feet
on sunburned stone, burrows deep
away from a sun just rising to meet a sky.
There was once in this dry place a sea
whose water blazed into flame,
ashed into white sand.
In the distance is the sound of thunder.
Perhaps a band of bipeds
may pass this way to drop small seeds.

At a Campfire

> "Come sit around the campfire, I will tell you
> a story" ~ Gabrielino Shaman

Great Spirit Kwawar looked down
to water and water and water.
where California wanted to be.
Turtle brothers, free in the waters
were listening
Great Spirit commanded them to come together.
Only after six days
turtle brothers obeyed Great Spirit,
lined up just so, looked like seven big islands.
Stay just so, said Great Spirit,
as he piled up rushes from the sky
over turtle's backs, scooped up earth in great piles,
made mountains on turtle brothers' backs.
Stay just so, said Great Spirit, then He said,
Those humps will make good mountains.
Great Spirit Kwawar stuck his fingers into the earth,
planted trees, let water seep up between turtle shells
to make lakes and rivers that ran to the sea.
Too much quiet made Great Spirit sad,
so he picked leaves from the new trees
blew on them, and they flew off singing,
Stay just so, said Great Spirit,
but the turtle brothers quarreled.

The new California began to shake and quiver,
a crack split the earth.
When turtle brothers
quarrel, when clouds quarrel, when people quarrel,
California shakes and quivers.

Stay as I made you, says Great Spirit.

NOTE: Quote after *Stories California Indians Told* by Anne B. Fisher

The Whisper

Sound fell from space
bouncing from
highest mountain tops
falling, blanketing
prairie and sea

The sound,
like a sweet whisper
to be decoded
by the upright walker.

For those who listened
the sound was warm
as though it had fallen from
somewhere far away

It splashed into lakes and rushed down rivers
people stopped what they were doing
to listen

They called the sound The Word

The singers began to sing it
but they couldn't understand
the words of the whisper
they made some of their own words

And worshiped them

The Music

The music fell, the little notes,
softly through night air,
dropping much like snowflakes
drifting everywhere.

The maestro must have dropped them,
or thrown them out (with care?)
I pick them up so carefully,
They're soft and light and fair.

I put them in my pocket
and pin them in my hair,
save them for the daytime
for singing, and to share.

But when I take them out and look,
the notes are lying there.
The maestro hasn't said yet how
to string them lest they tear.

I have those notes, a pocket full,
No others will compare.
Yet without the hand of the Maker
I must leave them there.

Back and Forth

The intrigue of time going backward!
Gertrude is shrinking now,
will soon take a lifetime away.
Steven will take knowledge,
Sophia her wisdom,
as Joseph took his unwritten words
into that backward journey
where old bodies become
younger each day. The old are born
from this world into that backward one
and fall filled and with a world
full with knowing and with doing
the veneer of experience thick
to follow the road into beginning.
After all the shedding away of years
baby bodies cry and suckle
rocked in a peaceful embrace
and knowing full well of love,
small bodies plump with beauty
press into breasts, reaching
into a 'new' one's beard,
a 'newborn's' wrinkled body,
smiling a smile until
an embryo curls into a pinhead egg
with one breath of life floating inside.
Perhaps not forward or backward,
but in circles.

Prophecy

She told me
when she was fourteen,
the age of certainty,
about the future.
For words she used
"rapture" and "tribulation"
and "Armageddon"
in sentences filled with
fearful scenes.
The prophecy unfolded.
There was the one great war
and the other,
another and another,
then the desert storm
that pitted every eyeball.
The earth shook and shook,
even while there was hunger
in the midst of famine.
She is forty today,
and with a smile
she says she no longer believes
the doom sayers.
We begin to talk
about asteroids
then think better of it.

Question

I once stood too close to an overhanging cliff,
fell into a deep canyon,
was impaled on a rotting stump.
Again, I was lost on a raging sea,
my boat was too small.
I was heaved into the sea, stored in a burrow,
eaten by eels.
Later, lessons learned, I hung on to trees
that I might not fall,
stayed far from the sea.
Is it best to be a shrinking coward, hiding?
I have learned the lessons.
So I hide.

Yes, I Grieve

Why are there no tears?
Inside my selfness
is the basement
where I keep
roiling pots, hot, bubbling
steaming, yet nothing spilling
no thick goo uncontrolled.
Each potion is known by color —
puce, burnt umber, faded yellow
grayed teal, washed-out black.
Why no tears?
Tears are light in weight
burn before they fall
cook beyond possibility.
On my pots are heavy lids
nothing leaks out.
Tears stay stored safely
in a safe place, evaporated.

Success, Fame

If I were a seedling hiding behind a weed
I would quietly grow, all by myself,
drinking in sun and rain,
dancing in breezes.
When I became a young weed
I would stand proudly at high noon
but never would I speak
My thoughts would be mine, I would miser them.
Other weeds would grow and blossom,
get pulled viciously from the ground.
I would be wise in my quietness. Yet,
I would not know the day
when beauty shone from me.
Not a weed, they would say
and they would clear space for me, to be seen.
But then I would not be hiding, thinking, growing
happy in the sun. I would be forced
to hold myself upright,
grow more leaves, endure the cut of the trimmer.
My pictures would be in the magazines
and people would try to steal me,
graft me, pot me, propagate me, clone me.
Soon I would see myself everywhere
and the seedling I was, the self I was to be
would never have mattered.

Chapter 2

Threads

A Long Thread

A thread hangs from an apple tree
that grows wide in a garden
unravels to a place outside
which leads to the filmy figures of gods,
to names like Kokhmah
and Binah, man and woman
to Shekinah, the rainbow
who gives her garment to Moses.
Threading to Isaac, Abraham,
the Saints, to the child of God,
and to Mother Mary.
The thread is looped through swords of crusaders,
around the thirst of Masada.
Always the thread turns red.
Allah, Adonai, Yahweh,
Jesus, El Senor, A Dios.
A needle threads
Gods and Goddesses,
silk around the Steel,
with bright coin tied on
here and there.
Great Spirits watch over all,
stitch with sinew threaded to bone
while ropes crisscross
over two poles
made from an unleafed tree.
A rough tapestry ... Just begun.

Threads, the Children

Eleven. Some began early,
have woven themselves
to the end of the cloth.
War. The thread colored red.
Fibers. The grey and black
shades of engines and tools,
aircraft and bombs.
Green field-twine lies decorated
with blue flax, yellow rapeseed.
Chokecherry-wine-silk
fills a decanter purple and sweet.
One yarn in the pattern,
a glittered thread, gold
catches a light near silver
which is tarnished.
A small coffined garment
still lies beneath lilacs.
The fabric of this family
is not yet complete —
still spins from spools
that lie dusty in a basket
at the foot of the bed.
Eleven children.
It is one more
than half-finished.

Thread, One

I.

Futile this search for beginning,
the shielding of eyes to see
the end of the dirt-brown thread
that connects him to him, you to you.

II.

Once, deep in a cave,
a child placed her hands
over the small prints of others
who had come before, a cave
large enough only for children
whose small hands
held a thread of lineage
wrapped around and around.
Yesterday, around and around
drew forth an unknown cousin
inviting her to the table.
Here is that thread, when pulled,
gathers a new love or an old friend.

III.

Life-colored fibers bring a child to your arms,
one child who will carry your days

into a new time.
No knot, one slim thread…

How long has it traveled
that piece of thread
come to rest beneath my shoe?

Voyage

Above 53 latitude
east and west of Greenwich
those I still remember
sailed into the Irish Sea
south of St George Channel
and weeks west through ocean
through churning Atlantic
or farther, where land
demanded one hundred miles
walking to the designated place

Her ships and his could have ridden
on seas side by side
if time had edged closer.
Now the children share
inside the 32 degrees
close to the earth's belly
on the great continent.

A hundred years or more it took
to travel those miles,
those many, many miles
due west.

Journeys
seem planned
whispered
by ancestors

Going Home

The road to home is far too long
Four lanes wide, covered with tar
Brittle in winter, melting in fall
Crowded with rushing car to car.

The road to home goes on and on
Desert and ocean passing my eye.
I have gone traveling miles too far.
I long to fly, pass others by
Though mired I am and longing to cry.

The road to home is a long black scar
Stretching and bending into a sky
And I have traveled much too far.

The journey home will be ending soon
And what will that ending be?
A soft clean bed and my own sweet world
New beginnings that will carry me
Into confusion of burdensome task
And the journey away will backward be.

Everywhere

water drips in a London flat
a canary sings in Paris
scree falls in Utah
falls on a silenced beetle
just one B flat howls in Sylmar
an intruder is caught
a stone skims on Lake Victoria
close to shore
thrown by a boy called Skip

water drips from a faucet in a London flat
everywhere there is movement
please that it shall never stop

a traveler, lonely, lodges with strangers
wind blows steady across the plains
Canada, the Ukraine
the first golden leaf falls
on still water
one pomegranate tree stands fruited with crows
rice paddies shine in moonlight
voices sing out camp songs in the tour bus
rain falls drop by drop on Paris fires
a tall man removes his tie in a Singapore hotel
a hungry woman eats lizard from a Beijing vendor
garlic fields are ready for harvest in Gilroy
a virus mutates in Gabon

a ball is thrown through a window
where there is no glass

water drips in a London flat
in Oz the wizard roars hiding the sound
of footfalls in the dark
water falls gently in a Tokyo Garden
rice steams in a bamboo pot
while a family breathes out breath
across the universe of ocean
to Ellis Island and the Pacific
in view of Liberty
on the Island of Manhattan
a whinny, a hoofbeat the call of fowl
from a dusty yard
water drips from a well bucket
sea jellies dance their rising and falling ballet
ma-ma-ma cries all over the world
the rector prays in a soft voice
mothers sing softly their lullabies
an echo from the cathedral choir
rises into treetops, disappears
ice rattles in goblets
dice crack against table sides
wine spills on a white cloth
as the ship rolls side to side

water drips in a London flat
"gone," say the nurses
a clock chimes

water pours to cleanse hands
white sand blows away
from Tasmanian shore
hot springs bubble in Iceland
a newborn cub cries feebly
a puma runt in a large litter
snow geese call, leave a wake of wings
flames roar in Paris

water drips in a London flat
supper outside is serenaded
by the whisper of wasp wings
one dead leaf falls in a Zen garden
on pure white sand
autumn bellows in Vermont
reds and yellows and browns
feasts for the eyes, blankets for seeds

water drips in a London flat
while we sleep.

Shawl

Over, under, over, under
one long weak thread
forms, the ends asunder
wrapped in knots.
New weaver in wonder
holds threads in her hands.

Over, under, violet, blue
the woof holds firm
the warp runs true
one long thread
up, down, through
silver, red, gold and blue.

After time and time and time
a fabric falls in splendor
weaver's fingers rough and worn
hold fine cloth, remember
every thread and every hue
not fashioned for the mender.

Keep warm, my child, she says
stand proud young shivering woman.

Smoke Rings

My father's curly black slicked hair
caught smoke rings blown through O-shaped lips
while mother sewed flowers
on pillow slips. She'd put the pincurls in my hair
as we sat together in the cool night air.

The smell of tobacco filled my hours
The men chain-smoked,
left worm shaped marks
in brown on woods in pairs.
Dishes flowed with ash, the women's mouths
turned bitter over black-ash cloth.

The grave lies open for my father's death
I curl his coat around and smell
the smoke rings tangled there
think of them over his curly hair
he left too soon. I loved him well.

Healing

It was her hands that healed.

Broth sustained, tomato juice,
cottage cheese, red jello

but it was her hands that healed.

Mustard fumes comforted, and camphor oil
the sound of her voice reading.

It was her hands that healed,
fingers over the eyes, a gentling back

stroking first the thin top hair,
caressing backward, tugging the braid,

becoming a warm hover of hands

like the touch of a prayer.
stroking again and again, her hands.

The child's body,
fevered and frail, felt the hands,

the hands that healed.

Who Is She, My Mother?

Who is she, my mother?
A brittle bough
with thorns
and silk flowers.
Who?
Brushing my hair every night,
custard pies,
a blue poodle-skirt hand-made.
She is
snow on a pot of stew,
ice on hot biscuits,
a silent supper.

Who is she, my mother?
Lalique and Haviland.
A fifty dollar tumbler brown
with good Scotch,
a paper napkin used for a week.
Who?
a voice reading Black Beauty,
all of it, when I was sick
and couldn't move.
She is
bee sting words,
hummingbird ears,
hands with fire on a sassy face.

Who is she, my mother?
Rose Point, a set of twelve
high-heeled slippers for lounging.
Her own parlor-maid.

Who?
A closet of garments,
the latest thing,
made by her hands for me.

She is
a small bird, frail and afraid,
stiff in her nest, grieving,
ready to take flight.

Who is she, my mother?
A tough roll of twine
rolled by hand by a Meacham farmer,
wanting to be satin ribbon.

Who?
Me. She is me.
Dust-free and polished.
I am my mother running.

She is
the strumming of my phone,
the conductor of my orchestra,
a wail of a sound.

Who is she, my mother?
A genius with wool and threads.
Oblivious to a poem.
Deaf to an idea not her own.

Who?
The one I used to know?
The one I know now?
The one I never will know?
The one I wish for?

She is
walking a road next to mine.
We talk.
But not to each other.
Who is she, my mother?
I don't know the mother of my heart.
I still search for her.

All About Ashes

It was said that Tamar
after the rape by her brother
was cast out and banished.
She wailed and covered her head with ashes.
Job, too, sat among the ash;
ash defined his sorrow.
Hear my prayer, my supplication, they said,
forgive my shame, soothe my sorrow, O God.
Ezekiel prophesized, wallowed in ash,
in dust on his hands and ashes in his hair.
Girded in sackcloth, they rolled in ashes.
Ash, the soft greyness left from a warming fire
from a meal where a family gathered.
Ashes, dust, contrition, sorrow, lowliness
as we all return to dust.
Yet my mother's ashes came merely
with her concern for simplicity.
A simpler task delivered with her love
and ours, scattered to make her free
and to free us as well.
Fuel, fire ash, ash, ashes.

My Mother Visits

She came to me as
Coyote
My mother —
A butterfly
To her son
My brother
Finally, I
Did see
She did understand
Her wild daughter
Lover of dirt and beast
Acknowledged!
In life, she stung and lashed
A girdle, no
A smaller one
Curly hair
Dresses
Dresses
Never wear jeans and always
Wear high heels
Set a proper table
Prepare a proper meal
Proper
Proper

Mother's Day 1998

We talked about
the deep black sea
where light patterns
years away
from the sun.

We talked about
jellyfish,
their slow dance
upward into green light.

We talked
of the new-found galaxy
until our taut minds
began to break.

That star we now see
has spun itself into planets
and fragments
in a place where time

bends backward
into our own beginning.

That evening
we stepped back
into ourselves
to this safe place of no time
this contortion
this skew, this warp
where we know it is always

now.

Take Me Away

Take me somewhere
the child said
as she lay there listless
upon her bed.

I took her to Africa
far away
to elephants, lion cubs
born to play.

Take me somewhere
she said to me
I rushed to do it,
but quietly.

We went to a barn
not far away
where the horses
stomped and chewed their hay.

Take me away
the little one said
curled herself up
upon the bed.

We went to the stars
far, far away

strolled the galaxies
day into day.

Take me somewhere
she whispered, then slept.
I closed up the storybook,
and off I crept.

Scent of Mystery

I can smell it coming,
the evening hug.
The scent is delicious.
My man comes home tired,
smelling of mystery
The scent that permeates
my life.

I could be smelling
refined bark or
herbs crushed in a mortar
or crystals brought to life
That scent that permeates
my life.

That lingered in my father's coats,
that comes through the dander
of my husband's galaxy
The breeze of yesterday
and today
The scent that permeates
my life.

It is the odor of
comfort and healing that
I smell, of potions
and thick creams,
syrups poured from
giant jugs,
mixed, emulsified,
to be taken for pain.

Tell me a Story, Daddy!

"Three little kittens, they lost their mittens,
then all began to cry. They stuck in their thumbs,
pulled out some plums and ate them
with green punkin' pie"
You got it all wrong, Daddy!
She laughed, clapped her hands,
shivered with joy as her dad told
his rhymes.
They are all wrong, she'd said
again and again, then he would smile,
repent, tell them all wrong again.
"One, two buckle your shoe,
I have to leave. It is true."
But three, four, I want more.
Busy man, builder of empires,
jailed in his world of work.
"Little Miss Muffet sat on a tuffet
eating spaghetti and rice.
Along came a spider, sat down beside her
said, Hello, aren't you nice?"
She would tell him a story next time.
*Talk to me, Daddy, sit with me,
tell me a story.*

Curiosity

> *"Only the curious have, if they live, a tale*
> *Worth telling at all."* ~ Alastair Reid

I watch her
cut chocolate milk
with scissors,
sprinkle the stones
with kool-aide,
pour water on sand
to watch it grow.
I listen as she talks
to an attentive crow,
wonder
what they know
that I do not.
I stop her when she climbs the fence
to peer over a precipice.

It hauled men
to the moon,
curiosity,
dissected bodies
in secret,
saw bats and frogs
inside a hollow tree,
curiosity, that fuel
that feeds
the hot fire.

I lay out the cards
again and again
to see if they will play
the same way twice.

Homecoming

Rainbows come in September,
winds about Christmas time.
That is, as I remember.

It's warm for the beach in November,
hills green up at the first of the year.
Yes I remember.

Leaves fall red in October,
brown heat at the end of July.
Yes, I remember.

I left the snow on white plains
when January was snowy cold.
It is that home that I remember.

I'll be back home in summer
when the fields are green.
It will be as I remember.

Great-Grandfather's Reply

Memories
are pushed on to me
in heaps
by my children
with pictures still and silent,
or colorfully moving about.
"Your life!" they say,
splendidly satisfied.
I smile my stiff smile
while boredom pushes
out of my body

Memories!
I have used them all
again and again,
have dusted, polished,
have put them away.
Now I wish to leave them
folded, where they are.

Take memories,
take them all, children!
Lay them in slick green bags.
I thank you.
For now I may empty out
the closet of my mind.
I have other things to do.

More than the Parts

My grandpa was three-quarter English and
one-quarter Irish. Granny was
All London.
That means Gram was one and two-fourths
English and one-eighth Irish.

My grandad was one half Hessian and
one-half something else, no one knows.
Gram was one-fourth English, one-fourth
Scottish and one-eighth Plains People,
Taptico was his name, the chief.
She is more than one-quarter missing.

That makes my daddy one-eighth English
and one-eighth Scottish and one-fourth Hessian and
one-fourth something else no one knows and
one eighth Plains People.

And I, then, am three-fourths and one-eighth
English,
one-eighth Scottish and one-eighth Hessian
and one sixteenth Plains People not to mention
one-eighth something else no one knows.
Now I know that I am twenty-one sixteenths
not counting the part no one knows.
I know who I am.
I am more than the sum of my parts.

The Landmark

At first glance you seem clothed in cement,
in broken windows, scattered stones,
in petticoats of leaves.
Inside, where your heart beats,
a scene paints itself on white walls,
marred by rain streaks, puddles —
a design like a diary of rainstorms.
Beneath arched doorways
float shadows of lovers,
of kisses beneath mistletoe.
Old castle, it is said, you were built
by a heartsick gentleman. His gift,
a magnet to lure a lady from France.
Today, under the sun —
no lovers' kiss, no mistletoe.
Men talk in the hollow, echoing vault
of space. A crowd outside waits
in seething rage. They will
try to tear you down. Old
you are and out of place.
Others stand before you,
their hands shield you.
Why do strangers see you as ugly?
Why are you in their way?
Your friends salute that man
that ghost of the lady from France.
Those of us — all who have loved
your beauty.

A Story

The house, now quiet and alone fills itself
with shadows which whisper from walls to walls,
which echo from halls to halls. It speaks in evening
to threaded vines wrapped around its doors,
to weeds in the long spent garden, to weeds
in the planks of floors. Memory peers in
from every room, collects in the darkened halls
lays dust in hardwood corners and on the echo
of songbird calls. Trees once knocked at the
windows, rain poured from a gabled roof,
children watched in the darkness, cold hail,
sleet and froth, while held in a grandfather's arms,
sung to by mothers and aunts.

The house remembers, it whispers,
breathes out with haunts. Our secret love still hides
behind broken bedroom shelves, we wrote
our names and signed them, just for ourselves.
Sad, there's no hoping for the place to stay,
to stand, to live on and on, for it soon will be
fallen down, and as time demands will be gone.
Someday the house will be buried
with grasses and sand and flowers.
All to be left, all to be found,
the memory of all those
living hours.

Chapter 3

Along The Path

New Year on Canvas

A new palette, blue-white,
Fresh brushes with no tint
That long season.
The whole last year
blanketed itself
over the backs of colors.

Those were the yesterdays
that mixed up to something odd.
Tubes of paint now lie fresh
not yet opened.

You are dressed in black
smart and slim
every day of the year.
and now I wonder
what your face would say
if I would give you
a sun-yellow sweater
edged in gold.

The new season has begun,
bright, clear and golden.
These are the days to remember.
Sunshine blue is a fine beginning.
Over that, a springtime tree.

Devil Wind

Devil wind drives hard the dust of morn,
Evil wind that dries the grass below,
Thirsty wind and hungry and forlorn.

Fragile shoots and blossoms newly born.
No chance of living after such a blow!
Devil wind drives hard the dust of morn.

This, the wind that touches earth with scorn,
The air that sucks out breath to grow.
Thirsty wind and hungry and forlorn.

Knife-blasts scrape, the face of earth is shorn,
Naked skin that pleads, adagio.
Devil wind drives hard the dust of morn.

May storm clouds roll along to shore,
Whip with rain-tears winds that go,
Thirsty wind and hungry and forlorn.

Close the doors against the wail, they warn,
Keep out choking dust and death, of woe.
Devil wind drives hard the dust of morn,
Thirsty wind and hungry and forlorn.

What the Thunder Said

dry grasses sang
in dry voice
a cappella
cracking
over high notes

seeds floated
on parachutes and
fell
on cracked sod

a dry sky gagged
on lightning forks
while
hot breezes made a santana sneeze

then the sun clouded over
thunder shouted with
dry
deep voice
commanding

"no more," he rumbled!
no more!
then he told
the rain to fall.

What Could You Do with a Bubble?

A child could see a rainbow in it,
A frog could be born.
Time could do something
Really special.
Waterbug could do his
Hunting, free to breathe,
While old men sit still to
Ponder its beauty.
A scientist could measure it,
Probing its mystery.
What could I do with a bubble?
I could watch it.
That would be enough.

Take it Back

The simple life, it is called and I shall try it,
not as simple as the sun in the morning
or the moon at night but less to polish, less to place,
fewer wonders to send for repair.
These sheets, one pair, towels two,
forks and knives and spoons
just one for me and one for you. No baubles,
three sets of clothing, one pair of shoes,
my make up bag, your shaving kit. But wait!
Maybe two sets of bedding and extra blanket.
And one more pillow. Oh, my mother's dishes
and our wedding stemware, well,
that wouldn't be too much. And the quilt
grandma made doesn't take much space,
and another pair of high heels. What if
company comes? Four place settings
and the playing cards. Checkbook, bills paid,
our transcripts and passports, and a desk
to put them in. And some furniture to store all of it.
But we will leave the deer head and the canoe.
The photos!? Scrapbooks? Our books and music?
Who will we be? What will my name be, yours,
if we have no stuff? Don't take it yet,
Mr. Rescue Relief men. I'll take it back.

Enlightenment

A dust devil blew in
from my childhood.
Dead leaves whirled up
from summer's hot soil
while a jay feather flew birdless
swirling into midsummer sky
up to the puffs of white cloud
as on the day when I was ten,
when I ran into the vortex
trying to find a secret
in the center of the whirlwind
only to rush away
with sand in an eye.
Sand still blinds me now.
Why does that thrill return
as the wind whirls in?
And why, now, do I run away?

Guilt

I think of the hours
of capricious killing
of earwig and spider,
of cricket and sphinx moth.
No longer does wolf spider
amble up the driveway
on a summer evening.
He is gone and she is gone
and all the babies.
The scriptures say
Thou shalt not kill.
Then they tell us
of heaven and hell
and hint at The Rewards.
I do not dare to dream
of earwig ghosts
and the afterlife full-bellied
with spider child and luna moth
and tomato worm and perhaps
even an occasional rattlesnake
to share my heaven with.
But alas, it is too late,
and I shall kill again
before I die.

The Grown-up Year

one day I saw wind
lying on the grass.
rain was locked up.

later,
my breath stopped to watch moonlight
lying golden on a pond.
little leaves
curled contentedly
to sleep.

autumn rejoices
with my soul.
Though I cannot join it yet,
I yawn and stretch,
getting ready.

Flowers

Lupines....
a gangly foal
dusty road
love

Sweet peas....
a little bouquet,
a new one born,
love

Roses....
One on the car seat
a dozen dried in a glass jar,
love

Yellow mustard...
a plaster,
soft hands and camphor oil,
love

Geraniums....
pulled from my garden,
muddy hands and feet,
love

Bouquets....
Mother's Day, Easter,
No reason at all,
love

Reveries

Enchanted
are the cottonwoods
Haunted
with the sound of a breeze
Magic
are the river rocks
Charmed
I am in my reverie
I wish
that I could ever be
Content
as flowers in the field
United
as the grass and trees
Captured
as to peace I yield

The Real Reason

Without milk, rain has
No flavor.
Without grasses, sunshine has
No taste.
Without grain, the wind is
But a wanderer.
Without flesh, the fire fills
No emptiness.
Without song, the air has
No purpose.
Without you and me, eternity has
No heart.
And God has
No reason.

As a Fly Buzzes by

In the office
At 3:00
Numbers
Fall nicely
Into place

This day is
3-3-88
How lovely!
The ledger shows 42.42 and
98.76

Fours are
Good and nice
Sevens are sometimes
Mean because they
Turn to sevens like
7. Eights
Get lost
On the bottoms
When I write them

Someday will be
9-9-99
The only one ever
Of its kind

The last
In a series
My work is ended
The day is over!
New to return
Again & again

Walls

High, no holds for a climb,
walls. Rough sides
that abrade, a paradigm
of bounds, to keep
out, as rabble, crime,

or in. Inside a wall
a climbing rose
A place to hide, to call
beneath the trees
to dream in silence,
see night fall.

I like a place
for a dog to roam
inside, to chase
with children safe
and, yes, the solitude
to hold the night's embrace.

I like piled stones
to grow against, flowers,
vines upon a fence.

Charlie remembers,
as a child shut out. Bolts
on the gates close tight
to keep the rabble out and fill
a child with longing, doubt.

The Glass

The glass,
the one we all know
as half-measure,
is empty, full, sits
on the end table
by the sofa.

Some of the water,
its life,
has been taken
by sun and air,
I left it there
too long.

Now that my need
for water
comes again,
my glass
is half empty.

I pour out
the remainder
into a smaller glass,
the blue one,
it fills to the top,
the very top,
with so much fullness
that a few drops spill over.

Catatonia — Stone

Cat a tonica, cat is a tonic, catatonica.
Like a stone, feeling nothing, oblivious
and innocent. I choose to be
a round stone in a fresh water stream,
giant granite on a crest.
When a trembling begins, in a rage
I fall to flatten enemies
into a bloody debris flow.

If I were a stone I would have no feeling,
no mouth, ears, eyes, no sense at all,
yet rock feels pressure
enough to break,
heat and cold enough
to flake,
gravity to pull from cliff to valley, broken.

Yet, I could be the one to hold up a wall,
the cornerstone of a home.
Catatonic, the stone which falls.
Cat is not a tonic for shattered sandstone.
Do stones feel? I could be a stone.

Collision

History is heavy here,
memory an intrusion.
Today is merely today
with nothing but the present!
Tujunga sun is granite sun,
crows caw with conviction,
children at school play loudly.
Pepper trees feel just a small breeze
while traffic turns right
onto Commerce Avenue,
beside my daddy's store.
I am hungry for ice cream.
No. That was long ago.
History and memory try to erase
the boundaries of this day.
I may go mad and raving
down to the boulevard
where a truck bears down
on its way to a razing.

Thought Fermentation

Something like sparklers
on the fourth of July;
words spurt, small fires
fire at night darkness,
fleeting, as unconnected
as our sentences.
I would like to speak to you,
but you have no ears,
only sparkler words
biting the night.

Cleaning Out the Past

this box is the past:
the patch of peeled paint from my closet, 1948,
a bale of cassette tapes, vinyl records,
reels of super 8 films, baby shoes, photo albums,
envelopes and boxes full of the words of lives.
To remember the past becomes tiresome;
the same baby's face in photo after photo,
puppies in a wagon, duck eggs in a stack.
To drift into the past to relive it; much too sad
for the pleasures do not return as yearned for.
Toss away three old houses and a beloved shop,
schools, churches, piano teachers,
Over there is the bottle collection,
gifts made by three year olds,
cake decorations of Jetsons and Flintstones.
Tempting, to rid all of it, all of yesterday,
all removed and retired. Oh, the space!
Two whole closets would empty,
the "unders," clear and dusted,
repaired and repainted, bare and shiny.
Space,
with only the present to fill it up.

Caged Things

Cuddly, well-loved, clean and fed,
the creature gnaws at the cage bars,
the bird flies in frenzy against a side,
tadpole butts its head on the side of the jar.
This is the way of all creatures,
coal miner, wife, child at school,
the man with ten children,
the wanderer,
this is the way
of all caged things.

Here I Lie Still,

quietly in my bed, warm
safe in the quilt
my Grandma made
still drifting in half sleep.
I concern myself
with filmy souls that linger
from dreams.
Fears collide with chaos.
I kick back at the pit
of my dream life
gray-striped life.
Yet, I don't wake, lie stiff
chilling to blue.
Without my chance
to grow old, to remember
all I did not do.
Never finished.
Am I not waking?
All I sorely now need
is the doorway
to find my way back
to repair
my sins of omission.

Chapter 4

Fallen Words

Puzzling

On a plank table large as a city
puzzle pieces, ten thousand
are placed, one for each day. In time
all the seas are formed,
the firmament of one piece,
trees and birds of the air.
Blue on blue on the tabletop,
forty years and it was done,
but one piece, two-out, two-in symmetry,
one gone somewhere, the verdant center
of a lone woman whose eyes stared forth.
After the search,
three lives later, the green-soul-center
was found hanging
on the sleeve of a threadbare sweater
abandoned for repair
now past claiming but for the poor,
the piece, plucked off, peered at
went bouncing on the way
to coffin in the city dump.
Her green soul. With no farewell.
Curious, there seemed too many pieces
before the puzzle was done.
The flat box stayed forever
on the top shelf, marked
"Good Puzzle. One piece missing."

New to New

1942

The scent of baking bread
rose early in the day
sounds of workmen
talking at the drug store
over coffee and a doughnut
the ringing of the bell
to call the children to school.

The druggist stood sleepy
from after-hours telegrams
delivered. Sad, about the boys
dead or wounded in the war.
Mrs. Jones and Mr. Lopez
finding out that way.
Doc had carried sweet peas along
for when the doors opened.

The new-paved street
was lined with stores
six on each side.
Groceries on credit?
Pay when you can,
I'll remember.

A wallet? Right here
where you left it.
It's all the money you have?
Here it is, not touched.

2029

All they need is your eyes.
Lines move quickly:
a picture, a touch on a
screen, a quick scan
at the check-out.
All they need
is the iris of your eyes.

How Far Have I Come?

shampoo for tinted hair
morning showers   river water
bubble bath   soapstone
                          leaves and grasses

stucco walls   damp caves
lath and paster   reed shelters
cotton sheets   soft hides

fireplace in a wall   firelit evenings
burning logs   singing a prayer
a book   the hunt

long night with fever   long night with fever
no breath   no breath
hospital   the dance, song, prayer

dozens of pills   tea from leaves
needles   potions
long life   time enough

childbirth pain   childbirth pain
love of one man   love of one man
the babies   the babies

cotton polyester   soft hides
dust   dust
a keyboard   a loom

I wonder   how close   is now
                   to then

Fibril Underneath

Twine that sticks to itself,
snipped threads' stubborn clinging,
wire encased in cable, wisps of hair
slicked in tight in pins,
silk winding like a shroud,
no end in sight, just wrapping.

Once words are said they begin
 to be true, even murmurs
wrapped in jokes or syllables
in small smiles, they get out and feed,
loom louder until they
plaster themselves to every surface.

The woman in sleek black
with crystals and a silver scarf
told me the one word about you
I did not know. Now which of us
will bear the secret that is
wrapping us so tightly

away from each other. You worry
about my acceptance,
I worry about my loyalty
and the words we will sew and sow.
Why did she say it,
that which no one wanted to hear?

Will that silken whisper become
a shroud to suffocate, or twine
too wet to untangle? Let your hair
blow free with the poisoned words,
shampoo them and scent them
with lavender, then sleep

until there is no more woman
in sleek black and crystals
whose words are no longer true,
merely remembered
like yesterday's novel or
last night's historical drama

covered in the confusion of fantasy
or reality poetry and prose.
We will all think we dreamed
the whole thing, we the watchers
steadying all we know of
the boundaries of the fabric
sewn beneath us.

Night Lights

Like a cat
swiping the window
in the darkness
a small sound, a tongue
letting in the night through glass.

Grandmother's bedroom
held a safe enough glow for sleeping alone
not bright enough to chase away sleep
yet fierce enough to scare monsters
hiding under the bed.

Bright enough one night to make
a seam clear around the blackout shades
shielding where my mother tended me
my sickness spread from blanket to floor
that light too small inside
too bright outside to please
the air raid warden as he passed by.

Tonight a twenty-five watt bulb guards
night wanderers
from ditches in rugs and walls that sway
even keeps the earthquakes away, yes
as a flashlight will do, from that room
which shook so hard January, 1994.

Outside in that black night
a thin moon shines
not enough light to save
a stumbling wanderer
who lost his slow way into a ditch
who was found cold and dead
in the sunshine of the morning

while the cat slept
Too much
Not enough.

Topography Map

I felt my grandma's softness,
felt her skin and loved it.
She showed me her arm
inside the elbow
where her skin was crinkly,
looked like the earthquake map
of California.
I saw hills and valleys
and the rivers of my grandma's life.
I clicked a picture
with my Brownie box camera
of my grandma's inside arm.
Developed, it showed only
an arm.
I am old too, now,
with crinkly skin.
This morning I photographed
my arm with a Canon DS126211
ran it through Olympus Camedia
printed out a 5x7
of my topography,
hung it on the wall.
Now that I am old like my Grandma
I am so beautiful.

Child on a Floor with a Marble

From the floor, peering into it,
the cat's eye seems larger
than his sister's sweater
lying on the sofa, larger
than the moon outside.

One small marble
in one small hand
eclipses the window, even a door.
In lamplight, the cat's eye,
set deep, glows orange
and alive, a pinpoint
of eerie otherworlds.

As the child's eye closes
he sees the center glowing
fire-like and the glass rolling
down a narrow hallway
to an open door, glass,
opens a mere crack,
inviting, maybe, freedom.

In dreaming, his body sweats
while he rolls unfettered,
unbound, free, sliding,
slipping further down in a dream
until the gentle tap;

"Son, come to bed now,"
and the sting of lost dreams hurts.

Sleep returns, deep and healing
not orange, just black.
In the marble's world
the cat's eye lies sleeping,
lost somewhere at the edge
of the front room carpet,
at the edge of outside.

I Missed You

I know someone
Who thinks
That days
Are made of people.
Some days
Are full
With bulges
But some days
Have rips in them
Or are empty.
Sad,
Isn't it?
I know someone
Who had
A Thursday
With a hole
In it.

I missed you.

Fallen Words

there were once crisp whispers
to mold us to each other
the sound of your voice in mid air

all the words have fallen
cry to be built again
with pen and spittle
tongue and teeth
yet, as they lie
nearly rebuilt
one upon another
words crumble to dust
pages crack parched
in the hand
down stairs of words
which fall slowly
to land in a dry heap
word puzzles dissolve
like sugar cubes
in a rain of glances
dry words
blown away by a cough
words
that cannot be pieced together
parchments that cannot be found
human sounds are grunts
only wheezing breath
heard in the night

New Box of Crayons

It's because there was no color
in that world
silver melted on the flatlands
gold puddled in the hollows
then one light day
cornflowers turned blue
trees dripped red
hills rose dandelion yellow
sky was a dome of asparagus green
eyes once grey glowed violet
It was because of the color
faces cracked, bodies shattered
minds oozed onto a palette
the master used a large brush
greyed the tones
caused the rains to fall
ash to settle
and let the wind blow free.

Echo

Would there be
some far-off world
where the call of a crow
would echo back
in the howl of a wolf?
Where a baby's first cry
would return
as an old man's laughter?
In the hills I called out my words
and they came back to me.
It makes sense
that the rocks
should call my name.
When they do,
when my words return
I hear my mother's voice
and the coughs and curses
of my father,
and all those whispers
from the ages past.
My own words?
I heard them flow forth
from my lips once.
Why would I want to
hear them again?
I would rather hear
an angel song
in clear high tones
or the call
of a meadowlark.

All This

A post with no fence.
A fence fallen down
a field, immense
unsold, unowned,
doors leading to doors
with no walls near
ceilings on floors
broken mirrors.
A high shelf
with nothing on it
one kiss lasting
for only a moment.
A place with no name
free admission
a hiding place, large
room for addition
in it a dance
with no steps
and in silence
songs without notes
sung in third tense.
Bird song
with no one to hear
a boiling pot
with no one near
a place to go when you die
unknown and unfound
Someone left. To cry
To cry.

The Word

A new word deposited itself on the page,
just born, fully formed, lovely and firm,
its meaning quite a mystery.
From the pen, above a blot of ink,
the word blazed in black.
The fading page sat for long years
waiting for translation.
Until the poet came,
washed off the dust,
rejoiced in its loveliness,
claimed it for his own.
Someone saw it,
wrote it in the dictionary,
made it real.

Darkness

In every eye, darkness —
The comforter embracing,
surrounding the weary
that each may be serene.

Once, there was blackness
over forest and seas
valleys and crossroads.
A vast universe out there
ablaze with austere stars
stretched farther
than any mind.

Let us not switch on a lamp
to cover the dark.
Lead us again and again
into the
holiness of night.

Captured from Henry Beston, *Outermost House.*

The Day the Poets Were Silent

Morning was misty with droplets on leaves.
Dewdrops made no difference, didn't matter.
Faces got washed, whiskers shaved away,
Children went off to school, the laundry got started.
By noon, mountains asked questions, like
Aren't I beautiful again today?
Mid afternoon saw a disturbance in mirrors, then
the mountains trembled, their little flowers shook.
People began to throw things and by dinner time
discussion erupted above the china plates,
the lamb roast, chewed without taste.
Milk soured and wine evaporated in the jug.
A hot evening hosted pacers, hand wringers,
phobics; the gangs brought out whole arsenals.
That evening's news had no meaning.
Moonlight's soft glow was cursed by insomniacs.
Firesides gave pale embers and ash.
Children cried, sent early to bed.
When the day was gone something strong had
escaped with it, something lovely, something sad,
Words had become for that day
merely words.

Love Poem

I'm acquainted with passion
(Infatuations from age five),
Years knowing unrequited
Unquieted
Love.

Why should I write a love poem?

Grandma told me
I should never kiss a man.
I would get blisters
And a baby.   Then
I read a book she had
Hidden under her bed,
And wished to become old.

Later I became young,
And lived the story.

Now my faded fingers write
A poem about love.

Why not?

If I Know Your Name

If I know your name
Will I know you, and you, me?
Butterfly, if I call you
King or Swallowtail,
Forest Nymph or Grayling
Will I know you?
Bird, if I shout Goldfinch,
Wood Thrush, Willow Wren
Will I know you?
Moth, are you Wooly Bear
or Death's Head?
If I call your names
Will you answer?
And if I tell you my name
Will you know me?

No Listing in the Yellow Pages

It is all here, bakers' supplies
flour mixes for bread machines
cell phones
dance with Pashkova
twenty pages for automobiles
seven for insurances
hobby shops and hypnotherapies
herbs and hot tubs in the H's
but the market is sluggish for
hippopotami, no listing, not one
in the yellow pages
gondola rides in Venice
kennels through karate
locks, lumber, travel,
tree service for the holy oak
turtles at Sees in chocolate
trophies, tropical fish

One could throw off the blues
get the impression that
all is well with the tender life
advertised in the yellow pages
party supplies, pest control
sculptured nails and ornamental iron
pet food warehouse, one hour photo
and physicians, Even 100 plumbers
skin care, sprinklers, swim pools
and shower doors, voice mail and
yoga at the end

Where Will I Put The Keys?

I sit here in this sweet place
a part of long ago.
The keys to open time hide
in little pieces of body cells,
in dust and in brittle paper,
lost.

Treasures gathered lie behind
locked places.
Treasures from another time
wait to be found.

This is the long ago, now, where
I am.
Where can I put the keys
for tomorrow so
my babies will
find them?

To The Stones

Boulder after boulder
pails full of stones
handled and dumped.
A cellar, hollowed out
a cistern, a well
a pile of rock
and one small hollow
in an empty land.
Stones, piled up
turned into walls
where winds could not enter
and storm could not pierce.
Floor, roof, it was finished,
the shelter, grown
from a rock-strewn field
into human habitation.
It had not been a simple task.
The rearranged rock
held secure a hundred years.
More. Walls to shelter babies
now grown, held
jars of fruit, barrels
of salt meat, tubers
stored in cool dark corners.
The people knelt,
grateful for those stones.

Bulky Item Pick Up

Today I am used up,
an object cast aside,
a bulky item, pick up.
I lie
with oleander trimmings,
with snake skin and old fur,
with dead leaves to be burned.
I leave
a whisper in the devil wind,
a touch wiped clean,
a kiss lost and never found.
I become
a heap in a landfill,
sustenance, for the children
of vermin,
a curse
on the mouth of
the open grave.

Chapter 5

Thunder Under the Ground

Two Times Around Is a Mile and a Half

I see footprints in the mud
In the path around the park.
My footsteps from the
Last time walking.

My feet now disturb dust.
Shatter the sycamore.
Crunch the squirrel's lunch.
Make thunder under the ground.

I follow the brown hard toes
Of the Gabrielino, the star-foot trail
Of blackbird, the thick-pad forefoot of
Coyote. My child's child

Walks barefoot in sand.
The seventh generation.
He looks up to empty sky where
There are no footsteps

But the one. How many times around
Is the mile to the moon?

The Fire that Drinks the Water

I hear thudding
fists on flesh. I see
red the color of anger
red of faces
blood red on broken hands

Anger, the red colored
consumes all emotion.
anger, the fire that drinks water
the red fire of anger

Spent, the madness flows
from red to grey
red to rust
to blackened ashes
drenched with rain

Anger, one human part
leaves stubble, ashes
rust-colored
patches of
snow

This Mad Journey

Time flows
in small streams
on my arm
ticking, flaking away
centrifuging with earth rotation
separating blood parts
into all one's selves
for transfusion.

If I knew the destination
of this journey of red
perhaps I would enjoy it more

Ripples

In my room I smell a cigar though no one smokes;
outside, ripples cover a still, clear pond
I know something makes those creaks
and passes beside my face, just out of sight.
That is the way of ghosts — a presence gone
from the water, from the room, my dad
smoking his cigar somewhere. Not here.

River Cutting

I mean no harm with my notions
spoken quietly, no orders
come from my voice. I work alone.
On the side of the road-cut
a brave trickle
works its way from deep in the mountain
persistently, quietly, a slow eroding
many steady drips; come, come with me,
we will join the company of waters it says.
Streams, rivers, torrents
that bring mountains
to their knees. I hope not to be
a river cutting through
causing too much change.

No, I *am* a river cutting. I apologize.

Color of the Mind

Those white birds, pigeons, I think
Trained to home; the elite of the sky!
Strange how the mind works
When scores of crows cruise
In the same direction
Black and gleaming, racing in flock
When they fly west at sundown
I see only evil

We once housed a cockatiel
White, yellow, lovely
When my hand entered its cage
Seed dish newly filled
It bit me
Every time

Oaks

A fine, good place.
A long straight road,
grass covered fields,
a wild oak wood,

a shady grove
sweet scented, cool,
one gentle slope
to a spring-fed pool

to lie beside,
to lay my head
on soft leaf pillow
a deep loam bed.

But the sound of the ax,
the sound of the saw
eats into my sleep
with its open claw.

and I arise, poise to fight,
I, inch high,
quaking with fright,
have fire in my eye.

The ax, the saw
don't see me there

as they hack the forest
clean and bare,
dress the wood
for table or trunk
for those who love
an oaken chunk.

I love the place
Where once the rain
fed the mountain
and fed the plain,
where acorns sprouted
and grew to trees
where the spring fed grove
caught late day breeze.

Now I lie
on a hard dry bed
Where the deep springs seep
and the oaks bleed red.

The Cremation of the Sycamore Tree

Never love the trees,
even though they sound
like wooden cymbals in a breeze,
a concert in an autumn wind.

Though branches decorate
the sky and make
the heart feel Deity,
never love a tree.

Never love a tree —
the one the children climb upon
whose limbs sit on a balcony,
whose mottled bark and golden leaf
join the sky. As one can see,

never love a tree.
Its roots uplift a road.
To fix that isn't free, you know,
nor pipes that break as rootlets grow.

Once an older sycamore
had evil ways which needed cease.
It took the men a day or more
to fell it, cut it piece by piece.

This winter its great heart
will warm us in the house

and we will hold a wake, a rite
to cause its spirit to arouse.

It's not wise to love a tree
that interferes with men.
Watch the smoke of sycamore form.
Smoke lifts as if to mourn.

Our hands and feet feel warm and dry.
Outside, a frosty elegy.
All because of that funeral fire —
the cremation of a sycamore tree.
We grieve, in honor incline our heads.
The tree turns to ashes
In its soft white bed.

All Beautiful and Treasured Things

I fly
over wild buckwheat,
desert willow, water birch;
sit
beside the cattails
and nibble them.
Above my head
flowers of ash branches
cover the sky
while western redbud
covers my eyes.

This is my place.
I walk
through Spanish broom,
creambush, touch the wild rose
while on my hair
puffs of cottonwood drift.
Snow plant is my morning
bedstraw my night.
My temple
stands among the flowers
of the chuparosa
beside the Lord's Candle.
I see mule fat and rabbitbush,
dodder and virgin's bower,

then after rain
the wildflowers:
lemon lily and fiddleneck.

All these treasures,
all names, so many names —
as many as rocks in a slide,
more than pebbles in a riverbed.
Not one can know them all.
Not every miracle has a name.

Sad that I can never greet them

                                without a name.

Prayer of Thanks

From dry crackling pathways
Stillness of overgrown chaparral
Comes that will to live.

Saws scrape at oak and spruce
Axes chop at the root balls
To clear an acre, to plant
To be warm and dry and fed.

From skins and meat
Feather and flesh
This guilty species grow,
First consumes

Absorbs, then becomes —
Deer and bear
Bush and root ball
Grass and seed

All of it
And then the prayer
Of thanksgiving.

Disaster

The wind is blowing, bar the doors
tornados are twisting, burrow deep.
When earth is trembling,
cower in the corner while whirlwinds
burn in the pines, run, run
a tempest is roaring, lower the sails
hurricane undermining, the ground is sinking
cliffs are falling, scratch at the walls
the sea is grabbing, eating the land
mud is pouring, get out, get out
people are washing away, the sea is calling
bar the doors, burrow deep, cower in a corner
run, run, no, scratch at the walls,
get out, get out, the wind is calling.

Viento fuerte, santana, berg, bora,
viable, foehn, norte, droshi,
sun downer, sirocco,
the Devil Wind.

The wind is coming again and again.

Memories

Watching memories take place
way back in them mind's cave
reminds me of flowers
arranged in a tall red vase.
Daisies and mums, dwarfed by zinnias
rise above fern and baby's breath.
Blue above, bright yellow below
they don't look right.
Now, yellow above, blue below
and a touch of orange — yes,
better this way.
Like memories which change shape
position this way and that
real or not, stay in the mind.
Those images from yesterday
those before knowledge
before language.
A look perhaps, a sound too strong
combines loud above, soft below
soft above, loud below.
I remember a face with gold teeth
I thought pleasing, and I always
look for that face in any crowd.
I remember. It was real.

A Cloud-Passed Moon

A cloud-passed moon
hangs steady
in the frame
of a cathedral rooftop
the same half-moon
which posed
behind fire flame
between Druid stones
in the frame of
a university window
where Copernicus lay.

It is the same moon
that heard the wolf's howl
that stroked the eyes
of sleepy shepherds
the same moon
which cast a spell
on a small-boned man
as he leaned
against post and lintel
It is the same moon
as it greets me now
full, in the frame
of a cathedral rooftop.

Spine Flower

I'm blue, so blue
This nightmare
Is no field of flowers
It is cactus, blue
That ripped my dreams
Tight off my back

Spine flowers live here
Horned ones, and they
Are in danger
Cannot be fed
Or sung to

Don't touch them
They bite
Don't bite them
They touch

Musings about Walls

There are many ways to build
a wall. Granite river-rock
piled up by a rule,
flat rocks vertical,
shouldered like a crowd lined up
old walls patchworked with moss.
Stone fences siding a field
mixed with bottles and boots.
Along the north side of the church at Naas
a door is marked. Once open
is now walled in
with unmatched stone
and its gate has a lock rusted closed,
clearly no accident. Think of this,
walled and locked doors
wrapping the church at Naas.
The poet says that there is
no neighbor who
doesn't love a wall, and walls
make good neighbors.
Think, what is being walled in
or out? A wall built with skill
is simply a lovely thing,
sculpted granite, piled stones,
an edifice in grey with green,
the setting for espaliered Bougainvillea.
Or an enclosure to keep something in.
Or out.

Rock, Bush, Sand

White sun beats down full-force
Furnace-hot as lizards bask
On warmed stone
A coyote pup noses in crevasses
Curious as I walk by
With no fear, he stares, trots away
A beetle lies still as the dead
Ignores my coming
Yet, far below, beneath sand
In a damp hollow, baby gophers
Nuzzle a mother, stilled
Waiting in kindness
I leave this place
Which is not my place

Sand, bush, rock

Blind-born Fish

If I were a blind-born fish
Pale and listless on a deep-sea cliff
Never to know the heat of sun
Nor the thin, white feel of day
I could never even dream of that
Called blue, called green, called warm
Nor visit a heat-scorched sand.

I see in this colored day
While sitting in filtered noon time sun
A world all full of blindness
And with the sight of all I know
I too am blind in some ways,
Like the blind-born fish on a deep-sea cliff
Content in the wonder of sightless day.

In Any Forest

It is plain why trees have eyes
Those scars where limbs have fallen
are like sockets that peer, that come
from some deep inside place;
pepper trees with bumps,
with growing tumors
and tangled hair.

At night they walk, the trees,
hoary monsters seeking,
as in any dream,
greater than the sum
of any part. Night terror.

In the daytime the creatures,
benevolent, offer shade
and a lacy bower,
eyes closed inside rough bark
It's all a chance of light.

Intersection

It was almost ominous
the child against a late sun
standing with arms outstretched
in joyous exclamation of life.
A cross made of child
intersecting the roads
earth and sky, mountain and air.

It was another time
when cross arms stretched out
in an exclamation of death.
A crossing, a crossroad
roads left or right for choosing
roads on seas.
Furled sails on crossed masts
across a horizon.
Intersection. Intimation. To choose.

A telephone pole to the right
holds a thousand voices raised
those crossed beams tell something
I don't know what.
Come, take this path to the left.
We will follow it to the corner.

Death Dances

Death dances best in a hot valley
where sand turns to glass
her filmy shrouds are called
horsetails up there in the sky.
She drinks the last drop of water
plays with life like a cat
with a mouse, laughs
curls up dry to stretch into a nap
while night birds sing
one more song.

Deep in the Spring

Winter lies where life
twists, wanders, meanders
vapor lifts upward into the sky.
We fly. Drops of rain fall —
a grand drink for field and tree
dew on clover, onto soft fur of a fawn,
on the down of baby chicks
the egg of frog forms from deep water,
from cloud billows
as earth drinks and drinks
until summer drinks all
though the spring is still deep.
Summer steals creeks.
Creeks tell all that life to sleep,
listen to leaves drop and crackle
earth shakes, earth bakes, earth falls down
to where down lies.
Grasses, beetles, toads
daffodils rest and sleep
in the bed where winter lies.
Deep in the spring rainwater waits
until the thaw, the surge of waters
that rage and flow,
purge the land until we become the sea.
We will be the sea.

My Very Own Place

I have it back again, this hovel in the wrong part of town.
Light green walls, white elbow-high wainscoting, brown

hardwood on the floors, much worn and pitted with living.
My own place, mine to furnish, not one item brand new.

Yes, I am selfish, my work life is over and finished.
I want and want yet. My riches, so far diminished

had no use. Is "mineness" a sin or salvation, I ask.
Forge the answer. I have before me a task: to create

a haven where I can hide, can be safe inside,
each flower and fabric I choose with pride

until it is finished.

I am lonely. Mine means just I.

This Romance

This pleasure
This love
Of water
Not opaque
No, but clear
Dyed soft blue by the sky
Not still but flowing
My hands make eddies
Waterfalls, pools
And I am mellow with
Delight
It is autumn
The owl cries out
Leaves dry and fall
Rivers, springs, dry
Small hollows, ponds

In the desert
Thirst is poised
As is the vulture
Winter comes here
But not rain
We go now
With our baskets and children
To the high country
The woods
A little water
Wait out the cold
Drink deep, the gift of
Icy water

It Wasn't Always This Way

Beneath these waters
pine stems sway
a sawmill rests
tools put away.

Ghostly folks
tend the stores
shine the windows
sweep the floors.

No longer needed
the timber town.
That's why this lake
is lying down.

Dammed up waters
for this richer place
and a world full of people
their thirsty pace.

The petroglyphs
the tribal ground
burying baskets
all are down.

Deep in this canyon
in the throat of this lake
the stream stopped up
a gentle wake.

Eating a shore
where coyote ate.

Chapter 6

The Web

Cards at Midnight

rows of cards undulate
aces to kings waving
lows to highs

outside the songs dance
waltz and barcarolle

hands place cards in waves
in a dance like rowing

slap, slap on tabletop
slap of wooden oars on water

as vapor covers the spots
worthless hands deal out
shuffling the night away
in their heads black stories
black truth like the petals
of The Dahlia

Green and Cresting

water rose in shades of green
the day we walked with bare feet
on the bottom of the sea

the day we saw conception —
whale, sea otter and butterfly
life still rushing on and around

to a beginning. Like the cresting
of the ocean waves, like the green fire
in that shiny place in the universe

like suns and the aurora, born
again and again like the bottom
of the sea, the place where we walked

Homeless

I bathe with earwigs
bubbly in the pink 50's tub
bug refugees that crept
from the watery mud
of wintry rainstorms
homeless earwigs slipping
upward on pink porcelain.
I think of rivers in gutters
of freeway underpasses dripping,
wonder where the homeless people sleep
these storm-swept days
even the homes built of bushes
are made of dripping leaves

Homeless…

Ant eggs will hatch soon
in underwater darkness
and I wonder if minnow babies will sprout gills
and if termites will keep their wings
and if there should be an ark
to climb aboard
in this rain-wet year
An ark for earwigs
and termites
ant babies

Thorns

I know the rose
The splendid rose
I know the thorns
The tender skin
I know the gash
The drops of blood
I know the fur
Caught on the thorn
I know the fur
I know the warmth
The noontime sun
The face of the rose
As it greets my eye
I know the rose
I know the thorn
The thorn I never touch
I leave no drop of
Fur or blood.
I know only the
Beauty
Of the rose.

Of the pure, the white
Rose.

Naming the Garden

Rose and Petunia. Lantana and Sage…
A passing breeze lifts my hair as I sit
pondering the beauty
of the life that surrounds me.
Bushes with plain and simple leafy life
reveal themselves and I speak their names
savor the sounds my lips make…
Xylosma, Sweet Jessamine, Plumbago Blue
Bougainvillea, Magenta, Fuschia,
bright yellow Palo Verde, iron-wooded and thorny
Wisteria surrounding it all to make me feel safe.
Leaves reflect sunlight as I name the flora.
Which is sweeter, the sight or the sound?
Words, wonderful words.
Sycamore, Pickeringia, Yucca, Fremontia.
Manzanita, Bay, Oak,
So many, so few.

That Day

So much happened on that day.
The elderly roses were discarded
those so long waited for
One purple iris stood defiant
while all the walls were falling down.
Pure water from the great vessels
fell into small-stoppered bottles
ran over, washed down
into sandy hollows

It was that day when thought itself
was attacked, set ways questioned
tradition taken apart to be examined
and discarded and one's own self
to be re-evaluated

That day so much happened —
lives were reassembled, the universe itself
redefined.
The water bottles taken back home.

NOTE: Earthquake, February 9, 1971

The Gallon of My Life

I have done well by my measure
Spoon by spoon, cup by cup
I have made maybe
A gallon

I carry my gallon of worthiness
Along with me proudly
Meet others whom I hope to
Impress

They don't think much of
My gallon at all
They show me their yardsticks
Then walk away with their
Measured pride

Wasp

One day, late afternoon
I felt the whisper of wasp wings
Wasp
Slender waist
Chest large to lean against
Long legs
A stinger poised
To bring a scream
Wasp
Her sisters
Trielis, Toltec, Pompilidae
Vespidae Mildei
Yellowjacket and digger…
The mothers
Flyers from north latitudes
Fathers from another continent
Their pale skin
Has defied the sun
Wasp
Whose homes are built
Of chewed wood and spit
Whose food is sucked from
Flowers and flesh
Supplied by lifetimes
Of toil and tedium
They speak in whispers
And pray
In their own words

Green

Green, they say, is jealousy
Green that I know is frothy sea
Teasing at the shore

Green is fragile springtime grass
Dancing in the breeze
Green, an unripe infant thing,
The promise of winter trees

Green, they say, is jealousy
A tear, and angry cry
I stand alone with feet stripped bare
Beneath a greening sky
Jealous of the green I see
Wanting more, and then
Waiting for the artist's breath
I find the taste of green again

The Web

The web holds me

Even though my hands
Are touching the power
Of a turbo-charged engine

The web still holds me

A junction beckons, draws me
Toward pine trees and streams
But my hand on the wheel
Is steady

The web holds me and
Will not let go

No — It is not the web that holds me

I am looking down and around me
At my captor
Once the web did hold me

Now
I am the web

The River of Time

What can be found in a river's past?
What seems to be lost? What now will last?
Boulders wash down from ridges and peaks
over wet pebbles into watery streaks
to pour into gullies and into ravines
to flow with the river, or so it seems.
What can be found in a river of days,
a river of memory of people's ways?
In summer a narrow river flows
near this town where soft wind blows.
Like drifting clouds we come together
on this fine day in July's hot weather.
We've gathered this day, have joined a parade
soon watch the fireworks blast, unafraid.
Night will spread on this river's face
fill first the hollows, the hidden space
until each shadow is captured by dark
and time has moved on. But first in this park
we dig up a river of time, of sorts
find out how life has taken its course.
We'll bury some trinkets, some hopes, dreams.
Rain will return, seep into the seams
Push pebbles and boulders into stony ravines.
yes, flow again with the river, it seems
over small pebbles into watery streaks
as boulders wash down from ridges and peaks.
What seems to be lost? What now will last?
What can be found in a river's past?

All the Way Down

Without prescription glass
the bottom is not clear,
only blurred shadows
in the deep crevasses
where all my moments have fallen.
Below are canyons full of hours
tinged with madness and elation
with riddles of living
and all the sodden questions
that lie in a heap.
I wish to fall, to purge deeper
that I may warm myself in the fires
at the center of earth
then stretching, hold Orion's hand.
And with my other hand
reach into the puzzle
of that fallen time.
This is a moment when flood waters
rise to the windowsill
streets on the map double
and blur into depthless rivers
and I am here, so shallow.
One more drop of rain
pooled in the hand of gravity
will wash me all the way down.

Now I Can Hear the Plodding of Beetles

There was once in this valley enough quiet
to make a public whisper. At night, owl called
and coyote sang her blessing over a meal.

From dusty trail the sound of hooves lent rhythm
to the melody of a wagon's wheels, a duet that entertained
midday. The old parson sag "Lord, I'm Comin' Home"
and the song was heard clear to the hills and beyond.

I have heard of silence deep enough to hurt the ear,
quiet, strong enough to hear the sound of blood rushing
and of heartbeat pounding. There was once a place where
murmured conversation could push away miles of silence.

In this valley, silence-gifted sounds of living
filled the air. Jays squabbled, springtime squirrels
chirped. Small creatures scurried, broke branches
and avalanched piles of pebble.

Now, so many years present, there is a deafness from noise.
Hammers tap duet with hand saw, a new orchestration.
A cement truck pounds sound onto the ready soil
covering the death cry of the horned spined flower.

Roaring as relentless as waterfall cascades
from the freeway, big rigs speeding, families rushing,
campers hurrying to quiet shores.

Over a rocky place beneath the asphalt of the 210,
empty flatbeds thump, bouncing over that stubborn place
where tough blobs of granite lay miles deep and three
inches too high. New echoes crush the sound

of mockingbird singing his song, of rodents scurrying
through brush. A cat's mouth meows. Sounds must come
from memory. Only in the mind is the call of mourning
dove and the sigh of breeze.

In my thoughts I can hear the plodding of beetles.

To J. Alfred Prufrock:

If I may be so bold,
I will not wear my trousers rolled,
but wear them scraping the ground,
listen to the scuffling sound;
the drag of leaf, the drag of dust
then see the pattern of brownish rust
as beauty of its own small kind.
It will not matter, I will not mind.

Chapter 7

Pillars of Motes

The Wind Is the Wind

Wind is a sea creature wan and pale
Playful, restless, chasing its tail.

It gathers fine friends out there in the sea
Breezes that circle capriciously.

Droplets of water jump up on their backs
They dance and they sing and they blow into cracks

Push up the clouds and churn up some waves
Gobble the sand that the seashore saves.

The wind plays in shallows and in the deep sea
Hiding its face so that we cannot see.

Or blows to a desert harsh and dry
Throws some dune-sand into the sky

Goes on to the forest soft and green
Wipes grasses and mountains fresh and clean.

Wildflower pollens on the fingers of breeze
Blow against rocks and sifts onto bees.

Or twists up the trees holding the soil
To slash and smash, to plunder and spoil.

It's hard to guess what the wind will do
Or breezes or currents as they pass through

But when they are finished, tired and fed
They shamelessly, slowly, creep home to bed

To sleep on top of the heaving sea
Wild wind, sweet wind, wind that is free.

After ...

Stained cloths clean and put away
floors stretch dust-free even into corners
gleam is the word for all of it
from mahogany to pecan
tea is hot — good to sip, good tea
Murphys from British Columbia
sunlight flows in from a westerly sun
holding pillars of motes

Dust to Dust

In that dry summer, after a winter of drought
few lupines blued fields, few poppies,
the chamomile lay low beside a path.
A hungry rabbit came hopping over the wall
for something green in a moist shaded corner.
As the sun poured itself low from the field's edge
it lay its light on one poppy, made it gleam,
that stubborn life wedged between two stones
on a hot, sunny wall. It had fought to live
with whatever was given it, flourished
to throw seeds for the next rainy year.
Died then, after all. Seed to seed.

Underneath

Seventy-seven floors
seven hundred rooms
seven thousand stairs
under that one desk
a list of things to do
like pick up clothes
where underneath
lay dust rolling
paper clips
a brief note about you
that says beneath your heart
is a memory of the times
we spent digging
down into the adobe
under the sagebrush
and under the rocks
where the rattlers live
underneath
where the earth is cool
and damp to our touch
in a dark place where we left
our games of heroes
our words of love, what might be
our past, down there deep
buried underneath.

Need the Light

I thought I would like the deep, dark woods
as I had loved the darkness around my sunlit home
the cries of the night.

In these midnight hollows I stumble, tree to tree
find nothing of comfort, no safety as tree bark scrapes
roots trip, the wind is no longer music
played through pines.

I need light for I feel danger lurking, heavy to bear
as I question the not knowing of eyes staring as I pass by
nor the thoughts born behind those quiet stares.

Yes, I need the Light for it is in the light that I see
loveliness, hear the songs and the sweet whispering
voices. At dawn the crows fly across the sky, dark-winged
ready to clean the world, as sunlight cleans
the deep dark woods.

The Old Ones, Gone Away

Life is short, he said,
for a wildflower.

His words did not stay death
nor change the span of life.

Time enough,
the poet said of the butterfly.

But just barely.

Some days are full of time,
some disappear in the mist
of the mind.

There is never enough.

No Words

The aching questions
lumped in her throat
where she pondered them
late that night.
Letters ran past
unconnected
with no meaning.
Trees swirled
beneath her feet.
There was no one
to listen
to her not-words
no faces
turned her way.
She spent that night
grabbing
at a runaway
alphabet
passing by
putting letters
in her mouth until
her lips were dry.
In the morning
some weeks later
she had them arranged
her name, his
even the names
of her nurses.

No Poem

Trees wall the river
Tall and green, with leaves
Big as pie tins and flowers
Yellow flowers that float
The sky dives so deep in the water
That down is brighter than up
We paddle upstream
Against morning sun, swerve
To catch blossoms, save them
As they turn brown on the prow
Down, the current cradles us
As it passes us beside taro fields
And forest hideaways made of
Coconut palms, mangoes and papayas

Let us rest our oars
No conflict is here
No story
No poem

I Wish for You

Safety from the waters and sinkholes
The shaking of earth and firestorms

Safe journey through the paths of leaders
Who threaten with stupidity and
Political paybacks

Water for the parched earth
Acorns and oaks
Bread

Shellproof bodies who labor
Comfort for those who grieve,
Friendship
That they may carry on

Spring grasses newly green,
Fields of alyssum that look like
Low clouds

Life again for naked burned hillsides
Bridges for sinkholes and washed-out gullies

I wish for you, for me, solutions, magic
Miracles, intellect, permissions

That may we solve

Maybe yes, maybe no

Hummingbird

take me with you,
picaflor,
>(four babies fit in a teaspoon),

>drink deep the deep nectar from the deep cup.

>>behind you the mountains stand,
>before you, flowers of sage and the chupa rosa.
dive,
>dart,
>>then fly,
>>>buzzing like the bee.

>>your colors shine in the sun and in my eye.
>colibri, picaflor, touch every blossom
as you fly.

>>Take me with you.

As Hawk Flies

There, as the hawk flies
I will fly,
As the Towhee calls,
I will call.
I will stir myself
Into the current of time
Where there are no days.
I will ride the Camel's Back
Into a galaxy,
Swim him deep
Into the pit of the sea
Where eels form the only light
And the fish are born blind.

Bury Me

with treasures;
a leaf from the cottonwoods
so I may take with me
that magic of the trees.
Place in my grave
the seed of an oak
so that I may hold heartwood
in my memory.
Put in a vessel of stones
from my beloved valley
that I will not become lost.
Leave in my hand
a feather from the road
that I may fly.
Then touch your hand
to my lips
that I may taste love
on my journey.

Yellow Tree Alone

Yellow tree
Stands glowing
In sideways light
Regal and glorious
Her beauty
Her message
For life's meaning
Wasted
With no one
To see that golden
Radiance
She sings
To no one
Who'd hear her
But to the Sun, Ra
The Giver of Gold

About Marlene Hitt

Marlene Hitt was the first Poet Laureate of Sunland Tujunga (1999- 2001). She has been a member of the Chupa Rosa Writers of Sunland- Tujunga and the Foothills since its inception in 1985. Her critically-acclaimed first poetry collection *Clocks and Water Drops* was published by Moonrise Press in 2015. In addition to publishing numerous poetry chapbooks, she has authored a non- fiction book *Sunland-Tujunga, from Village to City*. Her poems appeared in *Psychopoetica* (UK), *Chupa Rosa Diaries* of the Chupa Rosa Writers, Sunland (2001-2003), Glendale College's *Eclipse* anthologies, CSPS *California Quarterly* and *Poetry Letter*; three Moonrise Press anthologies — *Chopin with Cherries*, 2010; *Meditations on Divine Names*, 2012; and *We Are Here: Village Poets Anthology* that she co-edited in 2020 with Maja Trochimczyk. Most recently she was one of 12 poets invited to contribute to *Crystal Fire. Poems of Joy and Wisdom* (2022). Her work appears in *Sometimes in the Open*, a collection of verse by California Poets Laureate, and *The Coiled Serpent*, anthology of Los Angeles poets, edited by Luis Rodriguez (2016). She served at the Bolton Hall Museum in Tujunga as Museum Director and docent for many years. Ms. Hitt was the history writer for the *Foothill Leader, Glendale News Press, North Valley Reporter*, and *Voice of the Village* newspapers. She has been honored as the Woman of Achievement by the Business and Professional Women's Club, Woman of the Year by the U.S. Congress, and many congratulatory scrolls by the City and County of Los Angeles, and the State of California. In 2019, Village Poets of Sunland-Tujunga presented to Marlene and her husband Lloyd, a Lifetime Achievement Award, recognizing their support of poetry in the Foothills.

www.ingramcontent.com/pod-product-compliance
Lightning Source LLC
Chambersburg PA
CBHW071426160426
43195CB00013B/1819